By Sean Mendez

Foreword by World's Greatest Chef Ferran Adrià

Interlink Books

First published in the USA in 2011 by

INTERLINK BOOKS
An imprint of Interlink Publishing Group, Inc.
46 Crosby Street, Northampton, Massachusetts 01060
www.interlinkbooks.com

Library of Congress Cataloging-in-Publication Data available

ISBN 978-1-56656-866-1

Acknowledgements:
For all the children of Solidarity Sports, past, present and future. You are our inspiration.

Author: Sean Mendez
Production: Miriam Lovelace, Farrah Serroukh
Editors: Sarah Butler, Sophie Hull and Chris Brazier
Designers: Daniel Mendez and Ian Nixon
Cover design: Detlef Helmbold
Recipe Editors: Isabelle Lanoe, Rebecca Wright
Marketing Consultants: Ryan Bish, Hassan Laroussi and Dan Raymond-Barker
Facts Researchers: Samantha Briggs, Thando Thomas
Photographer: Andy Parsons (for additional photography credits see page 94).

Special thanks to:
Ferran Adrià, Zakiya Amlak, Ben Arogundade, Richard Cohen, Mirtha Diaz, Jorge Díaz-Cintas, Cliff Finn, Nuria
Gambau, Joy Lacdao, Sarah Linklater, Sandra Medina, Maria Mendez, Xavier Mendez, Jenny Mercurio, Javon
Middleton, Jane Milton, William Mcgranaghan, Sharni Raymond, Lawri-Ann Richards, Nisreene Akhrif, Anabel
Sánchez, Mirella Segura, Jermaine Shoy, George Vacoulas, Marco Pierre White, Octavia Foundation, Notting
Hill Housing Trust, Kensington Housing Trust, Dad's House, Looseleaf Productions, First Colour Printers, I Spy
Marketing, Latymer Christian Centre, Notting Hill Methodist Church, The Food Network.

Printed and bound in Italy

To request our complete 48-page full-color catalog, please call us toll
free at 1-800-238-LINK, visit our website at www.interlinkbooks.com,
or send us an e-mail: info@interlinkbooks.com

Contents

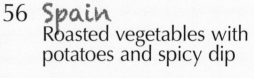
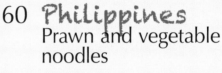

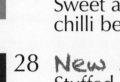

3

Ferran Adrià

Ferran Adrià is a remarkable chef. Born in Spain, he started off working as a humble dishwasher and recently won the award for Chef of the Decade. He was named in TIME magazine's 100 most influential figures of our time. His restaurant, elBulli, was voted best in the world for a record five years by Restaurant magazine. Every year, over two million people apply to eat at elBulli for only 8,000 places. However, maintaining such extremely high standards is exhausting, so Ferran has other exciting plans for the future. He aims to turn elBulli into a creative non-profit foundation and breeding ground for budding chefs to explore new ideas.

Ferran Adrià believes that food is the language of the world. We agree.

A dish from elBulli: pea jelly with banana and lime ice cream

Foreword

During the past few decades, our society has undergone profound changes which have brought with them new habits: statutory education, changes in family structure, financial pressures requiring both parents to work, etc. All of this means that there is less time to cook. As a consequence, our health has suffered. For the first time in history, we have gone from a period of food shortage to one of food surplus, although clearly, this problem is not one that occurs in the developing world, where tragically, thousands of people die of hunger every single day.

This new phenomenon of overfeeding, of an overabundance of products, together with the social changes I mentioned, has provoked a new health problem: the appearance, and expansion, of food-related problems, especially obesity, but also anorexia or bulimia, diseases which, in spite of our efforts, are growing. Even worse is that they are affecting the youngest of our population, starting with children.

If we do not find a solution soon, problems relating to unhealthy diets could become an unsustainable cost for most nations. We are living the contradiction that too much prosperity is leading us to a lower quality of life. That is why I always like to insist that investing in healthy food is the best investment we can make for ourselves, for our families and for the future. Also, healthy food is not more expensive and represents benefits that are felt in the short term. Only in this way will our youth and children truly know what well-being and quality of life mean. However, in order to do this, we (parents, doctors, cooks, teachers, etc.) must all lead the way.

Introduction

We spend about two hours cooking and eating per day. That amounts to more than four weeks per year, or over six years in a lifetime. So it is worth learning how to cook!

Cooking is a key life-skill

Modern lifestyles dictate that children spend many hours watching TV, playing computer games and on the internet. We are in danger of bringing up a generation who can't cook or don't have an interest in learning how to feed themselves. Childhood obesity has reached shocking levels. It is our responsibility to inspire children to live healthily. Children copy what adults do, so being passionate about cooking will rub off onto them. We must pass on those precious skills that will last a lifetime. A healthy child is more likely to become a healthy adult.

Cooking is fun!

Cooking and eating as a family is a rewarding bonding activity that will form some of your most cherished memories. Children love to cook and are naturally creative and curious. Each child learns at his or her own pace and with positive encouragement and patience, a passion for cooking can be sparked at any age. Cooking stimulates all the human senses, allowing children to become totally absorbed. Tantalizing the taste buds, watching your creation come to life, filling your home with the aroma of delicious food and the orchestra of sizzling, popping sounds are all part of an exciting culinary adventure.

About our recipes

Our recipes are not set in stone, so be creative and adjust them to meet your tastes. If you love garlic, use two cloves instead of one. If you are a fanatic, use five! Should you discover an amazing recipe, we'd love to hear about it: please email us on info@solidaritysports.org.

We encourage you to sit around the table as a family often and use it as a precious time to bond.

The most important ingredients in any meal are: love, bonding and sharing

Tips

Safety is crucial. Supervise young children closely at all times. Wear oven gloves if you are using the oven or touching anything hot. Remember to wash and dry your hands before cooking and after touching raw meat, fish and eggs.

Give children responsibilities. Children can start helping out at a very young age. They will thrive on being given a responsibility that is usually associated with adults. Creating a mess is fine; use it as an opportunity to explain that cleaning is an important aspect of cooking.

Assemble all ingredients. Set out all your ingredients before you start so that you do not have to search for any during cooking. Doing this also ensures that you don't forget to add any ingredients to your dish.

Taste as you go. Taste food often as you cook so you can adjust it to your liking and see how the flavors evolve. If it is bland, don't automatically go for the salt. A much healthier way to enhance flavor is to add spices, herbs or lemon juice.

Be adventurous. Don't be scared to experiment and be creative in the kitchen. Who would have thought that chocolate and chilli are such a delicious combination? If it works, great; if not, then you know not to repeat it and have learnt something new!

Chillies. Take care when using fresh or dried chillies. Rubbing eyes after handling can cause an unpleasant burning sensation. Wash your hands with milk, oil or lemon juice to remove the chilli.

Praise and eat together. Even if the outcome is not what you expected, congratulate the budding cook to give a sense of achievement. Families cooking and eating at different times means more work. Eating together is rewarding for all.

Make cooking educational. Ask your child to read each instruction aloud to develop their reading skills. Counting, weighing and measuring can introduce them to concepts of numbers, volume and accuracy. Children can learn a great deal without realizing it.

To the above, all you need to add is a dash of patience, a pinch of creativity and a heaped cup full of enthusiasm!

Notes

Recipes in this book are designed to be cooked by children and adults together. Adults should supervise children at all times. Tasks that can be performed at a particular age or stage in their development will differ from child to child. Most of the cooking methods have been simplified, but certain points might need to be explained.

All recipes in this book are designed to feed up to four people.

Where recipes include meat we have suggested a vegetarian alternative.

This book includes dishes made with nuts. Those with allergic reactions to nuts must avoid these foods.

Cooking times are provided as guidelines.

By pepper, we mean freshly ground black pepper to taste. By salt, we mean sea salt or low-sodium salt to taste.

All spoon measures are level.

Use unwaxed lemons when using the zest.

Cherry tomatoes can be replaced by any other variety.

Quantities in the images may not always represent those in the ingredient list.

We recommend using low-salt stock cubes without artifical additives or preservatives.

RUSSIA

Soup

Soup is a very important dish in Russia and it is eaten almost every day.

Caviar

Caviar is perhaps the most famous food exported from Russia; it is lightly salted roe or eggs of fish such as sturgeon, salmon and whitefish.

Fruity tea

Sbiten is a traditional hot drink for the Russian winter. It is based on a mixture of honey, water, spices and jam that are all boiled together and tastes similar to fruity tea.

Provide food

Russian proverb: "The rich would have to eat money if the poor did not provide food."

Boys unload bread for refugees in the Russian republic of Ingushetia.

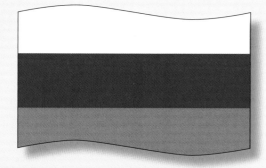

WHOLESOME SALAD

You will need

- 2 medium potatoes, peeled, diced
- 300g tin / 1½ cups cooked chickpeas / garbanzos, drained, rinsed
- handful green beans, trimmed, cut into small pieces
- 2 carrots, peeled, diced
- 2 hard-boiled eggs, diced

- 225g / ½ pound canned tuna, drained (optional)
- 225g / ½ pound jar of roasted peppers, drained
- handful green pitted olives, halved
- 3-4 tablespoons mayonnaise
- salt

14

1 Prepare the potatoes, carrots and green beans. Try to cut them roughly the same size so they cook evenly.

2 Boil potatoes, carrots, chickpeas / garbanzos and green beans in salted water for 10 minutes. Drain and rinse under cold water.

3 Place peppers, eggs, tuna (if using) and olives in a large bowl (leave some olives and strips of pepper aside for decoration).

4 Once all the water is drained, add the cooked vegetables and mayonnaise to the bowl.

5 Mix well. Decorate with peppers and olives. Refrigerate and serve cold or at room temperature.

6 As with any dish made with mayonnaise, it should be refrigerated and will not keep for more than 1 or 2 days.

Tasty tips *If you have the time, grill your own peppers. Grill whole peppers on a high heat until black all over and leave to cool. Peel, remove core and seeds and slice into strips. Crush a clove of garlic and mix with mayonnaise for a garlicky kick.*

15

BRAZIL

Feijoada

Feijoada is the national dish of Brazil and contains up to eight different types of meat. Feijoada contains all parts of the pig, including the tail, nose and ears.

Coffee

Brazil is the world leader in the production of coffee and provides around 25 per cent of the world's supply.

Barreado

Barreado, which means "muddy", is a typical Brazilian dish. It can take up to 24 hours to cook and contains many different meats and herbs.

Lemon

Many Brazilian dishes contain lemon. In Brazil the lemon is small and green, and is similar to limes in Europe.

Rafael Facarolo sieves coffee beans at San Benedito's Farm in Espirito Santo do Pinhal, Brazil.

SALMON STEW

You will need

Salmon stew
- 440g / 1 pound skinless, boneless salmon fillets, cut into chunks
- 400ml /1¾ cups tinned coconut milk
- 6 tomatoes
- ½ onion, finely chopped
- 1 red pepper, sliced thinly
- 1 yellow pepper, sliced thinly
- 1 teaspoon paprika
- 1 teaspoon shrimp paste
- 2 garlic cloves, finely chopped
- 2 red chillies, deseeded, finely chopped
- 2 tablespoons olive oil
- 1 lime
- salt, pepper

Brazilian-style white rice
- 225g / 1 cup long-grain rice
- ½ onion, finely chopped
- 2 garlic cloves, finely chopped
- 2 tablespoons olive oil
- 600ml / 2½ cups water

1 Add oil to a large pot. Fry onion, chillies, paprika, garlic and shrimp paste (if using) for 5 minutes. Season with salt and pepper.

2 Put tomatoes into boiling water for 1 minute. Drain and cool under running water. Peel, remove core and roughly chop.

3 Add tomatoes, peppers and coconut milk to pot. Cook for 5 minutes.

4 Add fish and cook for a further 5 minutes. Squeeze lime over the pot, cover and remove from heat. Make the rice by heating oil in a separate pot. Cook onions and garlic for 5 minutes. Add rice.

5 Mix well (stirring continuously so rice does not stick) for 2 minutes. Add water and cook according to packet.

Tasty tips *For a twist with texture, grill some cashew nuts until golden, crush and sprinkle over finished dish. The shrimp paste is optional and if hard to find, can be replaced with a dash of fish sauce. Pour in a cup of water in step 3 for a less rich dish.*

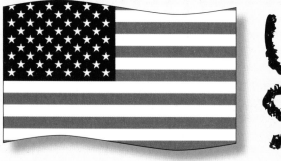

UNITED STATES

Distinctive tastes

The regional food of the United States is characterized by its extreme diversity. This is due to a combination of different cultures, traditions and locations.

Corn

The United States is the world's largest producer and exporter of corn (maize). About 20 per cent of the corn produced is exported to other countries.

Soul food

African slaves brought many of their native foods and cooking methods to the United States. Today, African-American food is known as "soul food".

Eat money?

A Native American proverb says: "Only after the last tree has been cut down. Only after the last fish has been caught. Only then will you find that money cannot be eaten."

NORTH AMERICA

SOUTH AMERICA

EUROPE

ASIA

AFRICA

AUSTRALASIA

A man picks apples at the Union Square farmers' market in Manhattan, New York, US.

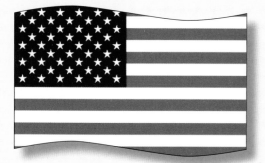

JAMBALAYA

You will need

- 225g / 1 cup long-grain rice
- 15-20 raw prawns (optional)
- 2 sausages, sliced
- 2 boneless chicken thighs, quartered (vegetarians could substitute canned kidney beans)
- 1 onion, chopped

- 1 red pepper, deseeded, chopped
- 1 stick celery, chopped
- 4 tablespoons tomato purée / paste
- 1 red chilli, deseeded, finely chopped
- 2 cloves garlic, thinly sliced
- ½ teaspoon cayenne

- pepper
- 1 teaspoon cajun spice
- 5 sprigs thyme
- 2 bay leaves
- 4 tablespoons olive oil
- 1 stock cube
- salt, pepper
- 600ml / 2½ cups water
- 1 lime, quartered
- bunch fresh parsley

1 Pour half the oil in a large pot. Fry the sausage pieces on high heat until brown all over. Set aside.

2 Season chicken (if using) with salt and pepper and fry. Some bits sticking to the pan is fine. Once cooked remove chicken.

3 Pour in more oil and fry onion, garlic and chilli for about 8 minutes.

4 Add celery, pepper, cayenne pepper and cajun spice. Cook for 10 minutes, stirring well. Add thyme and tomato purée / paste.

5 Cook for 3 minutes and then add the sausages and chicken (or beans) to the pan. Mix well. Add rice, water, bay leaves and stock cube.

6 Cook rice to taste. Add prawns (if using) 5 minutes before the end. Mix in parsley. Serve with some lime.

Tasty tips
Any sausage can be used for this dish – including vegetarian. You can replace the tomato purée / paste with fresh or tinned tomatoes. Try finishing the dish with a handful of fresh chives and a drizzle of olive oil.

CHINA

Snow

Ice cream was invented in China around 2000 BCE by packing a soft milk and rice mixture in snow.

Tea

Tea was invented in China and is an important part of Chinese culture. A Chinese proverb says, "better to be deprived of food for three days, than tea for one".

Chopsticks

Historically, Chinese people regarded knives and forks as weapons, so for eating they used chopsticks instead – and still do.

Chinese greeting

"Chi le mei you" ("Have you eaten?") is a traditional Chinese greeting.

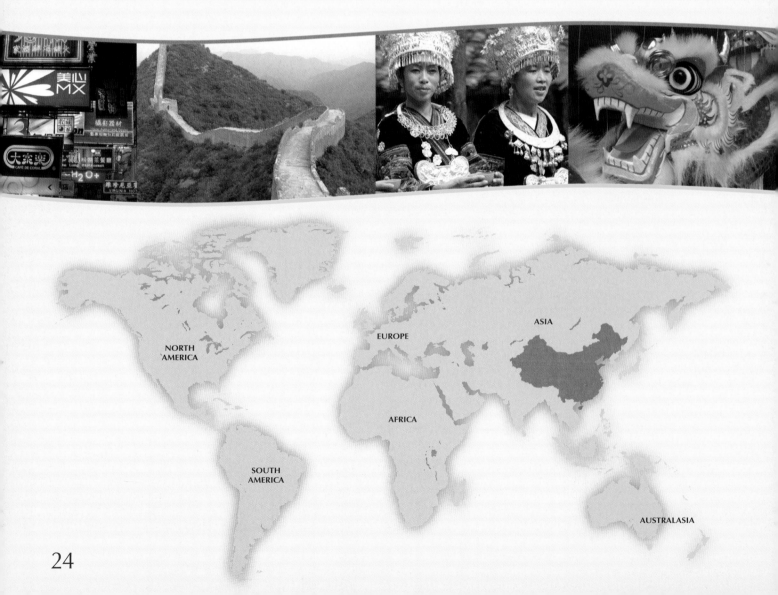

NORTH AMERICA

EUROPE

ASIA

AFRICA

SOUTH AMERICA

AUSTRALASIA

24

Five year old Gao Xin Yan enjoys a hot tea in Anqing, Anhui, China.

SWEET AND TANGY CHILLI BEEF SALAD

You will need

Salad
- 440g / 1 pound beef fillet (vegetarians can substitute tofu), cut into strips
- 2 handfuls baby spinach leaves
- 3 heads pak choi, washed, sliced
- 1 large ripe mango, cut into chunks
- 2 tablespoons sesame oil
- 1 teaspoon dried chilli flakes
- 2 tablespoons soy sauce
- pepper

Dressing
- 2 spring onions / scallions
- 2 tablespoons soy sauce
- 1 lime, juiced
- 1 orange, juiced
- 2 tablespoons olive oil
- 2 tablespoons honey
- 1 small cucumber, finely chopped
- 1 chilli, deseeded, finely chopped

26

1 Dressing: whisk together all the ingredients in a small bowl. Refrigerate.

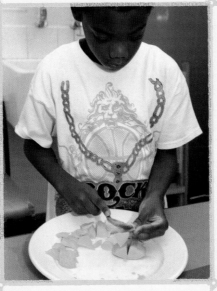

2 Prepare the mango by removing the stone, peeling and cutting into medium cubes.

3 Heat oil in a wok or pan. When hot, add strips of beef (or tofu) in a single layer, ensuring strips do not overlap.

4 Cook for 1-2 minutes on each side. Add chilli flakes, soy sauce and pepper while cooking every batch.

5 Scatter the spinach and pak choi over a large bowl. Spoon the chilli beef (or tofu) into the middle.

6 Sprinkle over the diced mangoes. Drizzle the dressing on top. Mix well and serve.

Tasty tips

A ripe mango should feel slightly soft. Using a ripe mango will ensure it's at its sweetest. Serve with bread to mop up the delicious dressing. Pak choi can be replaced by rocket or another leaf of your choice.

NEW ZEALAND

Sheep

New Zealand has a population of about 4.3 million people and 45 million sheep. That's a ratio of around 10 sheep per person!

Maori

The indigenous people of New Zealand, the Maori, call the country Aotearoa, which means "Land of the long white cloud".

National dessert

Pavlova, made with egg whites, cream and fresh fruit, is New Zealand's national dessert. It's named after the Russian ballerina Anna Pavlova.

Tradition

The Maori people bless their food or an elder says an acknowledgment before they start to eat.

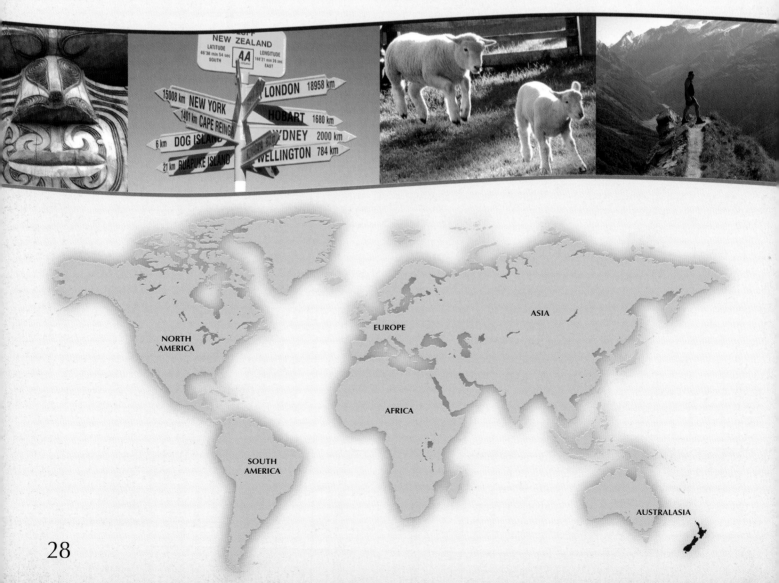

Local Maori children play on the beach at Scorching Bay just outside of Wellington, New Zealand.

STUFFED SWEET POTATO WITH GREEN SALAD

You will need

Sweet potatoes
- 4 sweet potatoes, cut in half lengthways
- 1 red pepper, diced
- 1 onion, finely chopped
- 2 garlic cloves, finely chopped
- 2 tablespoons olive oil
- bunch parsley, chopped
- salt, pepper

Green salad
- 1 baby fennel bulb, trimmed, core removed, thinly sliced
- handful baby spinach leaves
- handful watercress or rocket
- handful cherry tomatoes, halved
- handful seedless grapes, halved
- 6 tablespoons extra virgin olive oil
- 1 lemon, juiced
- salt

1 Preheat oven to gas mark 6 (200°C / 390°F). Score cut side of potatoes and brush with oil. Bake for 45 minutes or until tender.

2 Meanwhile, heat oil in a pan and cook vegetables for 15 minutes. Season with salt and pepper and stir often.

3 Remove potatoes from oven and scoop the soft flesh into a large bowl. Take care not to tear the skin of potatoes.

4 Roughly mash the sweet potato flesh. You may need someone to help you hold the bowl.

5 Add vegetables and parsley to bowl with mashed potato. Mix well. Spoon mixture into potato skins. Bake for 10 minutes.

6 Salad: whisk olive oil, lemon juice and salt in a large bowl. Toss in leaves, grapes and tomatoes. Mix well.

Tasty tips *Sprinkle tops of potato halves with cheese before putting back in the oven. Don't leave for too long, you want to melt the cheese, not cook it. Mix a little chopped garlic, soured cream and chives for a yummy dip for potatoes.*

INDIA

Side dishes

Traditional Indian food has only one main course (with rice or bread) served with a collection of savory side dishes.

Sacred animal

The cow is considered a sacred animal by many Indians who follow Hinduism, so beef is very seldom eaten.

Smoothies

In India, a smoothie is called a lassi. It is made by blending yoghurt with water or milk and Indian spices, often with fruit blended in too.

Sing their praises

An Indian proverb says, "Sing their praises, those who give you food."

NORTH AMERICA

EUROPE

ASIA

AFRICA

SOUTH AMERICA

AUSTRALASIA

Street vendor makes the traditional drink, lassi. Rajasthan, India.

CHICKEN and SPINACH CURRY

You will need

- 4 chicken breasts, cut into chunks (or 225g / 1 cup red lentils)
- 225g / ½ pound spinach leaves, washed
- 450g / 1 pound canned chopped tomatoes
- 1 onion, finely chopped
- 2 red chillies, deseeded, finely chopped

- 5-cm / 2-inch piece of ginger, peeled, roughly chopped
- 5 garlic cloves, roughly chopped
- 3 cardamom pods
- 2 bay leaves
- 1 cinnamon stick
- 2 teaspoons curry powder
- 2 teaspoons ground

- coriander
- 2 teaspoons garam masala
- 4 tablespoons plain yoghurt
- 2 tablespoons olive oil
- salt, pepper
- 225g / 1 cup basmati rice, cooked to packet instructions

1 Heat oil in a pot and add cardamom pods, bay leaves and cinnamon. Fry for 1 minute, moving constantly.

2 Add chillies, onion, salt, pepper and spices. Fry for 5 minutes, mixing often to ensure spices do not burn.

3 Blend ginger, garlic and tomatoes to a smooth paste with a blender. Pour in pot and simmer for 10 minutes.

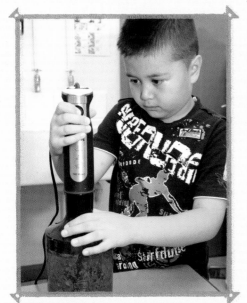

4 Blend uncooked spinach to a paste using 1 or 2 tablespoons of water to loosen. Remove cardamom pods from pan.

5 Add chicken pieces (or lentils) to pot and stir in the spinach paste (try not to spill it as we did!) Simmer for 10 minutes.

6 Remove from heat, add yoghurt and stir well. Serve on a bed of rice.

Tasty tips *Chicken can be replaced by lentils for a vegetarian and less costly meal. Finishing the curry with a squeeze of lemon adds a nice tang. If you prefer your curry stronger, use less yoghurt.*

35

TRINIDAD & TOBAGO

Influences

Trinidad's diversity is reflected in its cuisine with Creole, Indian and Chinese food being the main influences.

Peardrax

The pear-flavored soft drink, Peardrax, is very well liked in Trinidad. It is especially popular during Christmas, weddings and celebrations.

Coconut milk

Dishes from Trinidad are often stewed, barbecued, or curried with coconut milk.

Recipes

Unlike other Caribbean dishes, Trinidadian recipes do not often blend spices together: one taste or flavor usually stands out.

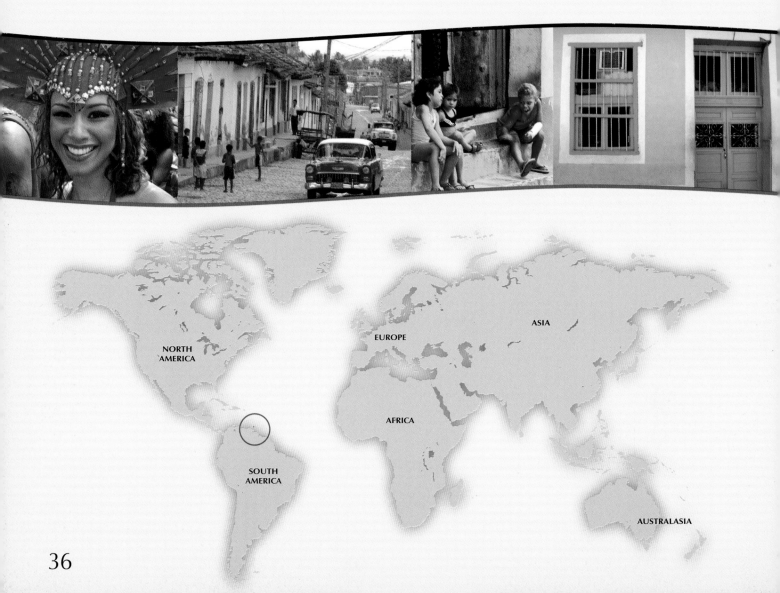

NORTH AMERICA

EUROPE

ASIA

AFRICA

SOUTH AMERICA

AUSTRALASIA

Excited boy runs home
with lunch for the family,
Columbus Bay, Trinidad.

MACARONI PIE WITH MIXED SALAD

You will need

Macaroni pie
- 225g / ½ pound macaroni pasta
- 150g / 6 oz cheese, grated
- 450g / 16 fl oz can evaporated milk
- 500g / 18 oz canned tuna chunks, drained (optional)
- 1 red onion, very finely chopped
- 1 red pepper, chopped
- 2 eggs
- 1-2 teaspoons chilli flakes
- salt

Mixed salad
- ½ iceberg lettuce, cleaned, ripped
- handful cherry tomatoes, halved
- 1 small cucumber, sliced
- 1 red pepper, sliced
- 10-15 olives, pitted
- 1 avocado, diced

Dressing
- 6 tablespoons extra virgin olive oil
- 2 tablespoons balsamic vinegar
- 1 lemon, juiced
- 1 teaspoon Dijon mustard
- salt
- a squeeze of honey

1 Preheat oven to gas mark 6 (200°C / 390°F). Boil macaroni in water according to time on packet. Grate cheese. Whisk eggs in a large bowl. Add evaporated milk, salt, onion, half the cheese, red pepper and chilli flakes.

2 If using tuna, drain can of water, add to bowl and stir. Drain macaroni and combine with the ingredients in the bowl.

3 Pour everything into a baking tray and cover with remaining cheese. Bake for 20 minutes until top goes crispy. If top does not go crispy, then put under a hot grill until it does.

4 In a large bowl, whisk all dressing ingredients. Add remaining salad ingredients to the bowl. Mix well.

Tasty tips *The dressing is very versatile, you can add a chopped chilli or change the vinegar and mustard for ones you prefer. Tuna is optional. Adding chopped tomatoes or carrots to the macaroni mix is another variation.*

39

MEXICO

Vanilla

Historians claim that vanilla, beans, coconuts and tomatoes all originally came from Mexico.

Corn

The most common ingredient used in Mexican food is corn (maize). Like the ancient civilizations from that region, Mexicans have learned to cook almost every meal with corn.

Spicy

Contrary to popular belief, all Mexican food is not spicy hot.

Food for the soul

Socializing and food are two of Mexico's most popular pastimes. A Mexican proverb says "Conversation is food for the soul."

Maya woman with a basket full of corn. Amatenango del Valle, Chiapas, Mexico.

FAJITAS

You will need

Fajitas
- 3 chicken breasts (or 400g / 14 oz tofu), cut into medium pieces
- 1 red pepper, cut into strips
- 1 green pepper, cut into strips
- 1 red onion, sliced
- tortilla wraps
- olive oil, as needed

Guacamole
- 2 avocados
- 1 tomato, chopped
- ½ red chilli, deseeded, finely chopped
- ½ lime, juiced
- ½ clove finely chopped garlic

Spice mix
- 1 teaspoon cajun spice
- 1 teaspoon onion powder
- 1 teaspoon oregano
- 1 teaspoon chilli powder (mild or hot)
- ½ teaspoon cumin

Tomato salsa
- 15 cherry tomatoes, chopped
- ½ garlic clove, finely chopped
- handful fresh parsley, chopped
- ½ lime, juiced

1 Spice mix: combine spices in a bowl. Salsa: mix salsa ingredients in another bowl. Refrigerate salsa to allow flavors to blend.

2 Guacamole: mash avocados with a fork. Add remaining ingredients. Mix well, cover and refrigerate.

3 Fajitas: in a large oiled pan, fry the chicken or tofu for 2 minutes each side. Sprinkle 2 teaspoons of spice mix evenly. Fry until cooked.

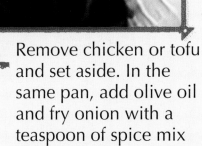

4 Remove chicken or tofu and set aside. In the same pan, add olive oil and fry onion with a teaspoon of spice mix for 5 minutes.

5 Add peppers and remaining spice mix to pan. Cook for 5 minutes, stirring often. Return chicken to pan. Mix well.

6 Heat flour tortillas and pile the mixture on top. Add the guacamole and salsa. Roll up and enjoy!

Tasty tips

Making the spice mix rather than buying a ready-made one makes a big difference to flavor. Replace chicken with tofu or leave out altogether for a yummy vegetarian dish.

MOROCCO

Mint tea

The most popular drink is green tea with mint. Traditionally, making good mint tea in Morocco is considered an art form, and drinking it with friends and family is an important daily ritual.

Medieval traveler

Ibn Battutah, famous medieval traveler and author, wrote of Morocco: "It is the best of countries, for its fruits are plentiful, running water and nourishing food are never exhausted."

Spices

The eight most important spices in Morocco are cinnamon, cumin, saffron, paprika, turmeric, black pepper, cayenne pepper and dried ginger.

Eat with hands

Moroccans almost always eat with their hands and use bread as a utensil.

NORTH AMERICA

SOUTH AMERICA

EUROPE

ASIA

AFRICA

AUSTRALASIA

A young boy selling fresh fruit
in Casablanca, Morocco.

COUSCOUS WITH CHICKPEAS AND PEPPERS

You will need

- 225g / ½ pound couscous
- 1 sweet potato, peeled, diced
- 1 aubergine / eggplant, diced
- 1 courgette / zucchini, diced
- 2 red peppers, diced
- 400g / 14 oz canned chickpeas /garbanzos, drained, rinsed
- 5-cm / 2-inch piece ginger, finely chopped
- 2 garlic cloves, chopped
- 1 teaspoon ground cumin
- 1 teaspoon ground allspice
- ½ teaspoon cayenne pepper
- 1 teaspoon ground cinnamon
- 1 teaspoon ground nutmeg
- bunch mint, chopped
- handful raisins
- 2-3 lemons, juiced
- 500ml / 2 cups water
- olive oil, as needed
- salt

1 Prepare the vegetables. Heat some olive oil in a large pot. Cook aubergine / eggplant potato, ginger and garlic for 5 minutes.

2 Add a little more olive oil, salt and all the spices. Cook for about 5 minutes stirring well. Be careful not to burn the spices.

3 Add chickpeas / garbanzos, peppers, courgette / zucchini, and water. Cover and simmer for about 8 minutes. Stir occasionally.

4 Add lemon juice and couscous. Stir, cover and remove from heat.

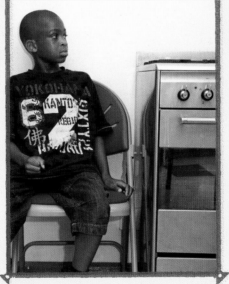

5 Allow couscous to sit for about 10 minutes or until it becomes light and fluffy when mixed.

6 Add raisins, mint and mix in. Drizzle with olive oil and enjoy.

Tasty tips
Soak raisins in orange juice for 1 hour before adding to dish for delicious, plump raisins! For a fruity twist, add small pieces of dates and dried apricots – treat like raisins.

COLOMBIA

Coffee

Coffee is Colombia's biggest agricultural export and is considered worldwide to be of the highest quality.

Delicacies

You may find delicacies like roasted ants in one part of Colombia, which wouldn't be eaten in another part of the country.

Time

Some Colombian recipes require a lot of time, like the traditional dessert Arequipe, which must be mixed for 4 to 5 hours until it gets thick.

Tradition

When going to a Colombian's home, it is considered polite to bring fruit, a potted plant or chocolates for the host.

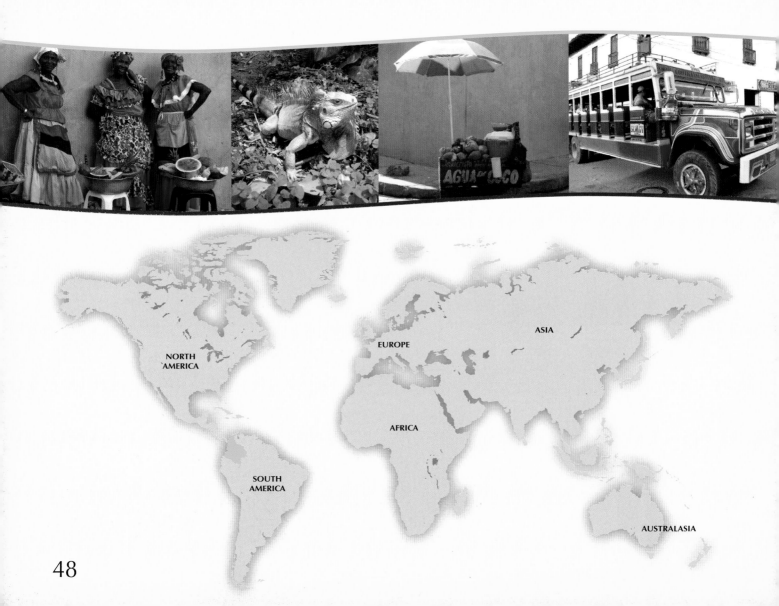

NORTH AMERICA

EUROPE

ASIA

AFRICA

SOUTH AMERICA

AUSTRALASIA

Woman on her way to selling fruits in Cartagena de las Indias, Colombia.

CREAMY AVOCADO SOUP WITH GARLIC BREAD

You will need

Soup
- 2 leeks, sliced
- 1 large potato, peeled and diced
- 500ml / 2 cups milk
- 1 avocado, mashed
- 1 tablespoon fresh chives, chopped
- 1 vegetable stock cube
- 600ml / 2½ cups water
- 2 tablespoons olive oil
- salt

Garlic bread
- 1 baguette French bread
- butter
- 1 clove garlic

1 Heat the olive oil in a large pot. Add leeks and salt. Cook for 5 minutes, stirring well occasionally.

2 Add potato, water and stock cube to pot. Simmer until soft, about 10 minutes. Remove from heat, allow to cool a little.

3 Off the heat, blend vegetables with a hand blender. Carefully stir in the milk and allow to cool further.

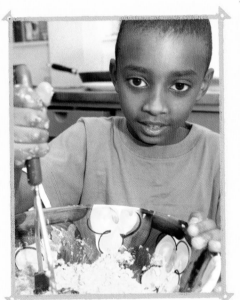

4 Meanwhile, mash the avocado until smooth. You can use a masher or a fork for this.

5 Add avocado to pot and then blend gently again. Pour soup into bowls and decorate with chopped chives.

6 Cut the bread in half longways. Toast cut side. Peel clove. Rub onto cut side of bread. Spread a thin layer of butter.

Tasty tips *You can eat this soup at room temperature or chilled. Ensure you allow it to cool before adding the avocado as heat embitters the avocado. Drizzle with extra virgin olive oil just before serving to add a nice velvety texture.*

SOMALIA

Halal

Cuisine in Somalia is Halal. This means that food is prepared in accordance with Islamic dietary guidance.

Canjeero

A popular main dish in Somali is canjeero, which is a small pancake-like bread. For children, canjeero is mixed with tea and sesame oil to encourage growth.

Snack

A sambusa, a Somali version of the samosa, is a popular snack. It is spiced with hot green pepper and the main ingredient is often ground meat.

Perfume

Somalis traditionally perfume their homes after meals. Incense is placed on top of hot charcoal inside an incense burner. It burns for about ten minutes, keeping the house fragrant for hours.

Young girl in Kebribeya, Somalia.

RICE WITH VEGETABLES

You will need

- 225g / 1 cup basmati rice, rinsed
- 1 onion, finely diced
- 3 garlic cloves, peeled, finely chopped
- 2 courgettes / zucchini, diced
- 2 peppers, any colors, diced
- 1 carrot, peeled, diced
- 1 vegetable stock cube
- 4 cardamom pods
- 4 cloves
- 1 cinnamon stick
- 1 teaspoon ground cumin
- 1 teaspoon ground turmeric
- 1 teaspoon curry powder
- 600ml / 2½ cups water
- 4 tablespoons olive oil
- salt, pepper

1 Heat half the oil in a large pot. Fry onion and garlic for about 8 minutes, stirring often.

2 Add cinnamon stick and spices and cook for 3 minutes to release their flavor. Pour in the rest of the oil.

3 Add the remaining vegetables. Season with salt and pepper. Cook for 5 minutes, stirring occasionally.

4 Rinse rice until water runs clear. Add rice and water to pot, crumble stock cube in and bring to a simmer. Cook rice according to pack instructions.

5 Remove cardamom pods and cloves, if you can find them!

Tasty tips *This dish is also nice finished with a handful of juicy raisins or your favorite fresh herb. For those addicted to spice, sprinkle some Tabasco over your dish and tuck in!*

SPAIN

Siesta

After lunch in Spain, many people rest or take a nap. This is called a "siesta".

Rabbit

In northern Spain, you are more likely to find rabbit served in a restaurant than chicken.

Tapas

Tapas is not a type of food but a way of eating it. Tapar means "cover" and tapas was traditionally a slice of cheese or ham, placed over a drink to protect it from flies.

Wine

Spain is the third largest producer of wine in the world, behind Italy and France. A Spanish proverb says, "For wine to taste of wine, you must drink it with a friend."

NORTH AMERICA

SOUTH AMERICA

EUROPE

ASIA

AFRICA

AUSTRALASIA

A fresh pile of fish at
La Boquería market in
Barcelona, Spain.

ROASTED VEGETABLES WITH POTATOES AND SPICY DIP

You will need

Vegetables
- 2 aubergines / eggplants
- 2 large onions, cut in half, skin on
- 3 red peppers
- 4 tablespoons extra virgin olive oil
- salt, pepper

Potatoes with spicy dip
- 3 large potatoes, skin on, diced
- 250g / ½ pound passata / tomato paste
- 1 onion, finely chopped
- 2 garlic cloves, finely chopped
- 2 tablespoons olive oil
- ½ teaspoon cayenne pepper
- salt, pepper

1 Preheat oven to gas mark 8 (230°C / 450°F). Brush vegetables with oil. Place in the oven for about an hour, turning occasionally.

2 Place in a covered bowl until cool – the steam will help loosen the skins. Remove skin, seeds and core from red peppers.

3 Peel skins off onions and aubergines / eggplants. Slice peppers and aubergines / eggplants and arrange on platter.

4 Drizzle vegetables with extra virgin olive oil. Add salt and pepper. Delicious served at room temperature.

5 Dip: Fry onion and garlic in oil for 5 minutes. Add cayenne pepper, cook for 3 minutes. Pour in passata / tomato paste, simmer for 5 minutes.

6 Potatoes: Boil potatoes for 10 minutes, drain and pat dry. Fry in oil until golden brown. Season with salt and pepper.

Tasty tips *If your onions have not caramelized well in the oven, then fry them, cut side down, on high heat for 2 mins. You might have to fry the potatoes in two batches to ensure they get crispy.*

59

PHILIPPINES

Coconuts

The Philippines are the largest producers of coconuts and coconut oil in the world. The coconut tree is considered to be the 'Tree of Life'.

Porridge and chocolate

Champorado is a common breakfast enjoyed in the Philippines. It is a type of rice porridge flavored with chocolate.

Fork and spoon

Food is eaten with a fork in one hand and a spoon in the other; knives are seldom used.

Water jar

A Filipino proverb says, "Don't empty the water jar until the rain falls."

NORTH AMERICA

EUROPE

ASIA

AFRICA

SOUTH AMERICA

AUSTRALASIA

Children search for the
sea urchin delicacy on
Malapascura Island,
Philippines.

PRAWN AND VEGETABLE NOODLES

You will need

- 600g / 20 oz egg or rice noodles
- 15-20 prawns or 4 boiled eggs, diced
- ½ small cabbage, sliced
- 1 onion, sliced
- 3 spring onions / scallions, sliced
- 3 garlic cloves, chopped

- handful mangetouts / snowpeas
- handful baby corn / candle corn, halved
- 1 carrot, peeled, grated
- 2 sticks celery, diced
- 2 red chillies, deseeded, finely chopped
- 1 stock cube

- handful cashew nuts
- low salt soy sauce
- 4 tablespoons oyster sauce
- 2 tablespoons sesame oil
- 2 limes
- pepper
- 500ml / 2 cups water

1 In a large pot or wok, add the oil. Fry onion, chilli and garlic for about 8 minutes. Season with pepper.

2 Prepare corn, cabbage, carrot and celery. Add to pot and cook for 10 minutes, stirring well.

3 Add the mangetouts/snowpeas and mix well.

4 Add water, oyster sauce and stock cube. Simmer for 3 minutes. Mix in noodles and prawns. Cook for 3 minutes.

5 Carefully grill nuts for a few minutes until light brown (those above are a bit burnt!) Crush with pestle and mortar.

6 Add lime juice (and egg pieces if using). Sprinkle with sliced spring onions / scallions and crushed cashew nuts. Add soy sauce to taste.

Tasty tips

If using fresh noodles, there is no need to add water/stock. You can use leeks instead of onions and try replacing the prawns with chopped sausage.

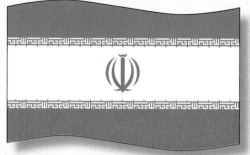

IRAN

Ice cream

Iranian ice cream often contains frozen flakes of clotted cream. It is sometimes flavored with the refreshing combination of saffron and rose water.

Mind and spirit

Iranians believe that eating should nourish the mind and spirit as well as the body.

Rice

Rice is a staple food and the Iranians cook it superbly. It is often eaten with wheat bread, yoghurt, lamb and aubergines / eggplants.

Persian

Iranian cuisine is often referred to as "Persian". This is because, until 1934, Iran was known as Persia.

NORTH AMERICA

EUROPE

ASIA

AFRICA

SOUTH AMERICA

AUSTRALASIA

Five-year-old Setayesh
enjoys an ice cream at the
Garden Museum of Art in
Tehran, Iran.

KEBABS

You will need

Kebabs

- 400g / 14 oz lean lamb steaks or tofu, cut into 2.5-cm / 1-inch chunks
- 3 peppers, any colors, cut into 2.5-cm / 1-inch cubes
- 16 cherry tomatoes
- 16 small mushrooms
- 8 pitta breads
- bamboo skewers
- 2 tablespoons olive oil

Marinade

- 1 lemon, finely grated zest and juice
- 2 garlic cloves, finely chopped
- 1 teaspoon dried mint
- 1 teaspoon dried rosemary
- 1 teaspoon ground cumin
- 1 tablespoon olive oil
- ½ teaspoon cayenne pepper
- salt, pepper

Yoghurt dip

- 225g / 1 cup natural yoghurt
- 1 tablespoon freshly chopped mint
- squeeze of lemon
- salt, pepper

66

 1 Put bamboo skewers to soak in cold water. Mix all the marinade ingredients in a bowl.

2 Massage lamb or tofu with marinade, cover and refrigerate for 1 hour. In a bowl, season vegetables with salt and pepper and drizzle with olive oil. Then thread the peppers, lamb or tofu, mushrooms and tomatoes alternately on to the skewers.

3 Make sure you pierce ingredients through the middle so they don't fall off during cooking.

4 Drizzle skewers with oil and cook on high heat for 3-4 minutes each side. To create a char-grilled effect, use a griddle pan.

5 Yoghurt dip: mix ingredients together for an easy delicious dip for the kebabs! Serve with grilled pitta bread.

Tasty tips *Marinade the lamb overnight for full flavor. You can replace one of the vegetables with courgettes / zucchini, which are delicious grilled in this way. Try to cut all the ingredients the same size so they cook evenly.*

67

AUSTRALIA

Lamingtons

Lamingtons are an Australian specialty: they are square sponge cakes coated in chocolate and shredded coconut and often served for afternoon tea.

Aboriginal people

Traditionally, Australia's Aboriginal people worshipped their land. They hunted only what they needed to eat and gathered plants and roots to sustain themselves.

Barbecues

Modern Australians are well known for their love of barbecues which are an integral part of their culture. The hot climate is perfect for enjoying an outdoor feast!

Poem

Aboriginal poem: "We don't own the land, the land owns us. The land is my mother, my mother is the land… The land is our food, our culture, our spirit and identity."

Aboriginal women hold fruits, nuts and berries. Tjapukai Park, Queensland, Australia.

FISH PARCEL WITH DAMPER BREAD

You will need

Fish parcels
- 4 white skinless, boneless fish fillets
- 16 asparagus, stalks snapped off
- 1 red onion, thinly sliced

- 12 cherry tomatoes, halved
- handful fresh lemon thyme
- 1 lemon
- olive oil
- paprika
- salt

Damper bread
- 250g / 2 cups self-raising flour
- 80g / 3oz parmesan cheese, grated
- 1 sprig fresh rosemary, just

leaves, chopped
- 150ml / 5 fl oz milk
- salt

1 Preheat oven to gas mark 6 (200°C / 390°F). Sift flour and salt in a large bowl. Add rosemary, cheese and milk. Stir well and make into a round shape about 7.5 cm / 3 inches thick. Place on a lightly oiled baking tray and bake for about 30 minutes.

2 Lay 4 pieces of foil on a table. Spread with onion slices. Place each fish fillet on top of the onion, add asparagus either side.

3 Add salt, paprika and lemon thyme. Place tomatoes on top of each fillet. Drizzle with oil and a squeeze of lemon.

4 Wrap fish in foil. Ensure corners are turned up so juices are not lost. Be careful not to pierce foil with the asparagus.

5 Cook in oven for about 15 minutes. Serve with juices from the foil, adding some more lemon juice.

Tasty tips
Add a teaspoon of butter on each fish fillet before folding the foil. The butter will melt in the oven and form a mouth-watering sauce with the olive oil, lemon and fish juices. Add the thyme both under and on top of the fish. Finish with a fresh herb.

UNITED KINGDOM

Sandwiches

The sandwich is named after the fourth Earl of Sandwich. He once ordered meat between two pieces of bread to stop his hands getting greasy while he played cards.

Salt

Food in Tudor times was heavily salted to stop it going bad; the salt disguised the taste of rotting meat.

Diverse

The British are known for their love of foreign food and have one of the most diverse food cultures in the world. Chinese and Indian dishes regularly top the polls of the nation's favorite dishes.

Luck

Hot cross buns are made at Easter and are sometimes kept as luck charms.

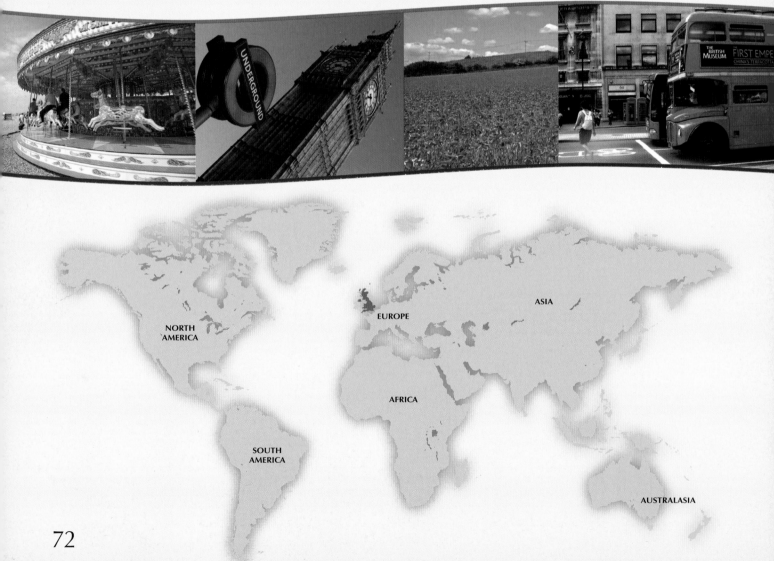

NORTH AMERICA

EUROPE

ASIA

AFRICA

SOUTH AMERICA

AUSTRALASIA

Boy eating ice cream at Glastonbury Festival.

SHEPHERD'S PIE

You will need

- 2 tablespoons olive oil
- 450g / 1 pound minced lean lamb (vegetarians can use soy mince)
- 1 onion, finely chopped
- 2 carrots, peeled, grated
- 2 celery sticks, finely chopped
- 2 cloves garlic, finely chopped
- 4 tablespoons Worcester sauce
- 5 sprigs fresh thyme
- 1 stock cube in 250ml / 1 cup water
- 1 star anise
- 1kg / 2¼ pounds potatoes, peeled, cut into chunks
- 50g / 2 oz butter
- 150ml / 5 fl oz milk
- 2 egg yolks
- 100g / 4 oz cheese
- salt, pepper

1 Heat half the oil in a pan. Fry all the vegetables for 10 minutes, stirring well. Set vegetables aside.

2 Add more oil. Increase heat. Fry lamb (if using) for 5 minutes, breaking up any big lumps. Drain lamb in a colander. Return to pan.

3 Return vegetables to pan and mix well (add soy mince now, if using). Add stock, thyme, star anise and Worcester sauce. Simmer for 20 minutes.

4 Meanwhile, boil potatoes until soft, about 15 minutes. Drain well and return to hot pan. Allow to dry for 5 minutes.

5 Preheat oven to gas mark 5 (190°C / 375°F). Add warmed milk, butter, egg yolks, salt and pepper to pan. Mash until smooth.

6 Transfer mince to baking tray and flatten. Add potato on top and sprinkle with cheese. Bake for 15 minutes.

Tasty tips

Mix in half the cheese when you have finished mashing the potatoes. Try adding mushrooms or some tomatoes with the vegetables. This dish is even more delicious the next day.

75

GHANA

Cocoa

Ghana is one of the world's largest suppliers of cocoa. It also produces a variety of tropical fruits such as mangoes, papayas and coconuts.

Bowl of water

Traditionally a bowl of water is provided at the start and end of the meal for people to wash their hands.

Into a ball

Food in Ghana is scooped and formed into a ball with the right hand before being eaten.

Ghanaian proverb

A Ghanaian proverb says, "Nature gave us two cheeks instead of one to make it easier to eat hot food."

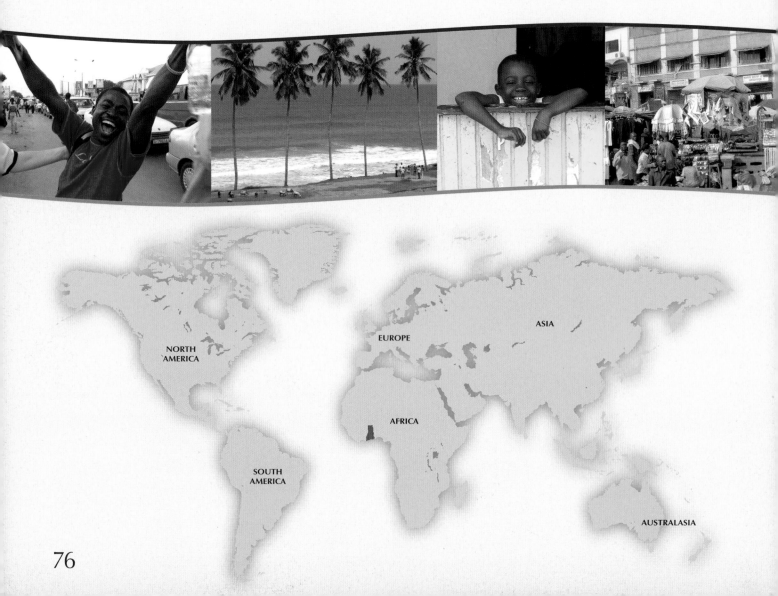

NORTH AMERICA

EUROPE

ASIA

AFRICA

SOUTH AMERICA

AUSTRALASIA

Cocoa farmers ferment and dry cocoa beans in the blazing sun in Diaso, Ghana.

JOLLOF RICE

You will need

- 300g / 10 oz beef, cut into chunks, or 400g / 15 oz canned kidney beans
- 225g / 1 cup long grain rice, rinsed
- 400g / 14.5 oz can chopped tomatoes
- ½ small cabbage, shredded
- 1 red pepper, diced

- 1 onion, finely chopped
- handful green beans, trimmed, chopped
- 3 garlic cloves, finely chopped
- ½ tablespoon cayenne pepper
- ½ tablespoon curry powder
- 5 sprigs fresh thyme

- 2 bay leaves
- 1 stock cube
- 4 tablespoons olive oil
- 600ml / 2½ cups water
- salt

1 Pour half the oil in a pot. When hot, fry half the meat until brown and set aside. Repeat with remaining meat (if using beans, miss this stage).

2 Add oil, onion, garlic, salt and spices. Fry for 8 minutes, stirring often. Add red pepper and cabbage.

3 Then add tomatoes and green beans. Cook for 10 minutes, stirring well occasionally.

4 Pour in the water. Place the bay leaves, thyme and crumbled stock cube into the pot.

5 Add rinsed rice and browned meat. Bring to a simmer and cook rice according to pack instructions.

6 More water might have to be added to cook the rice.

Tasty tips *The variations of this dish are endless. Try adding mushrooms, carrots or aubergines / eggplants. The meat can be replaced by fish such as prawns or crab as well as by beans.*

GREECE

Apples

In Greek history, throwing an apple to a girl was a traditional way of proposing.

Lamb

The favorite meat served in Greek homes and restaurants is lamb, which is sometimes spit-roasted on an open fire.

Tsoureki

The traditional Easter bread, Tsoureki, has a slightly sweet flavor. Greeks also make Easter cookies to share with friends and family.

Olive oil

The average Greek person consumes more olive oil than anyone else in the world, over 26 liters (7 gallons) per year!

Men separate olives from leaves before pressing. Amiras, Crete, Greece.

FETA SALAD WITH TZADZIKI

You will need

Salad
- ½ large cucumber, diced
- 1 small red onion, thinly sliced
- large handful cherry tomatoes, halved
- handful Kalamata olives
- 225g / ½ pound feta
- 1 cos lettuce, torn
- 1 red pepper, sliced

Dressing
- 6 tablespoons extra virgin olive oil
- ½ garlic clove, finely chopped
- 1 teaspoon dried oregano
- 1 lemon, juiced
- salt

Tzadziki
- ½ large cucumber, peeled, deseeded, finely diced
- 250g / 1 cup Greek yoghurt
- ½ garlic clove, finely chopped
- bunch fresh mint, chopped
- 1 lemon, juiced
- salt

82

1 Tzadziki: mix ingredients in a bowl, removing cucumber seeds as above. Taste! Adjust and refrigerate.

2 For the salad, whisk all the dressing ingredients at the bottom of a large bowl.

3 Add the red onion to the bowl. The dressing will 'cook' the onion and remove its harshness.

4 Wash and prepare the cucumber, tomatoes, pepper, lettuce. Drain and remove pips from the olives. Add to bowl.

5 Crumble in feta cheese. Mix well to ensure dressing does not stay at the bottom of the bowl.

6 Serve with crusty bread to dip in tzadziki.

Tasty tips

You can finish this salad off with some freshly chopped mint, parsley or basil. Replace lemon juice with your favorite vinegar and try adding a splash of olive oil to the tzadziki.

JAMAICA

Marinade

Jerk, a spicy dry-rub or marinade for meat, is now one of the most popular Jamaican foods worldwide.

Ackee

Jamaica's national fruit is ackee. It must be eaten fully ripe or cooked or else it is poisonous.

Breadfruit

Breadfruit is usually roasted and eaten for breakfast. It was introduced to Jamaica from Tahiti in 1793 to provide food for slaves.

Fiery

Scotch bonnet peppers are a vital ingredient in jerk sauce. There are over 200 varieties of this fiery pepper.

Chef proudly holds up a piece of jerk chicken, Riu Montego Bay, Jamaica.

FISH CAKES WITH RICE AND BEANS

You will need

Fish cakes
- 450g / 1 pound skinless / boneless cod or haddock
- 100g / 3.5 oz flour
- 1 onion, finely chopped
- 2 garlic cloves, finely sliced
- 2 eggs, whisked
- 1 teaspoon curry powder
- 1 teaspoon allspice
- 1 teaspoon cayenne pepper
- bunch fresh parsley
- 1 lemon, juice and zest
- olive oil, as needed
- bay leaf
- salt
- milk, to cover fish
- 100g /3.5 oz breadcrumbs

Rice and beans
- 400g / 15 oz can red kidney beans
- 225g / 1 cup long-grain rice, rinsed
- 1 scotch bonnet pepper, pricked
- 600ml / 2 ½ cups water
- 5 sprigs fresh thyme
- salt

Salsa
- 1 mango, finely diced
- 1 pepper, finely diced
- 1 spring onion / scallion, sliced
- 1 red chilli, deseeded, chopped
- 1 tablespoon fresh coriander / cilantro
- 1 lime

1 Place fish and bay leaf, in a deep frying pan. Cover with milk and simmer for 10 minutes, Drain and flake into a large bowl.

2 Salsa: mix ingredients, refrigerate. Fish cakes: fry onions, garlic in oil for 5 minutes. Add spices, salt, cook for 5 more minutes.

3 Add onion, lemon zest, eggs, breadcrumbs and parsley to fish bowl. Mix well. Shape into round cakes. Coat well in flour.

4 Rice: place rinsed beans, pepper, rice, water, salt and thyme in a pan. Bring to a simmer.

5 Cover and cook rice according to packet instructions. When cooked, remove pepper.

6 Fry the fish cakes in oil for a few minutes on both sides until golden and crispy. Serve with wedges of lemon.

Tasty tips *If mixture falls apart easily when shaping, refrigerate for 20 minutes. Add breadcrumbs or mashed potato to fish mixture for more body or to make more on a budget. You can replace the fresh fish with canned fish.*

10 fabulous smoothies

Smoothies are a great way of ensuring your family gets their five-a-day of fruit and vegetables. If you prefer your smoothie thicker, use yoghurt or add a banana. If you like it less creamy, replace milk with fruit juice. It's your choice. All these recipes make two healthy portions.

Below are some helpful tips – although the best tip of all is to use your imagination!

Use fruit that is ripe and in season – that way it will taste its best and cost less.

Vegetables are great in smoothies. Spinach, kale, carrots, peppers, cucumbers or celery are just some of the nutrient-packed foods that are worth using.

Try freezing smoothies with a spoon in your cup or yoghurt pot. Remove from freezer, twist, and you have a healthy ice lolly!

If you are using canned fruit, make sure it's in natural juices or water and not syrup.

Add the liquids to the blender first to avoid the fruit binding up the blade and getting stuck.

It's fine to use frozen fruit in your smoothie. Though try not to freeze in a big lump or it will be hard to separate.

Even if you don't have the exact ingredients listed, give it a try anyway and have some fun experimenting!

STRAWBERRY DELIGHT

- 10 strawberries   • 1 banana   • 250ml / 1 cup milk

A delicious, classic combination and family favorite. A complete treat.

MANGO SUNSET

- 1 mango   • 1 banana   • 10 raspberries   • 2 oranges

Don't waste the mango around the stone. Chew and suck on it unashamedly!

BLUEBERRY BURST

- 60 blueberries   • 1 banana   • 1 kiwi   • 250ml / 1 cup milk

Ensure the blueberries are ripe so they are at their sweetest.

GRAPE DREAM

- 1 banana   • 40 grapes   • 1 stick celery (with leaves)   • 250ml / 1 cup milk

An explosion of well-balanced flavors. Grapes and celery are a wonderful mix.

PEAR PASSION

- 2 pears   • 1 carrot   • 250ml / 1 cup unsweetened apple juice

This drink is bursting with healthiness. The subtle pear taste is divine.

RED
ORANGE

- 3 oranges • 1 apple • 20 raspberries

A tangy pink fruit juice with bundles of flavor and energy. Try adding a squeeze of lime.

PURE
WATERMELON

- Works well with any melon

Mouthwatering. Try leaving the seeds in for more vitamins and a nutty touch.

PASSION

- 2 passion fruit • 2 bananas • 250ml / 1 cup unsweetened apple juice

The tart passion fruit adds an exotic taste that is not overpowered by the apple juice.

CREAM
PEACH

- 3 peaches • 250ml / 1 cup milk

Peaches and cream are a dream combination, nothing else needed.

MAGIC
BANANA

- 2 bananas • 2 tablespoons desiccated coconut • 250ml / 1 cup milk

A creamy drink with the exquisite tropical taste of coconut. Try adding passion fruit.

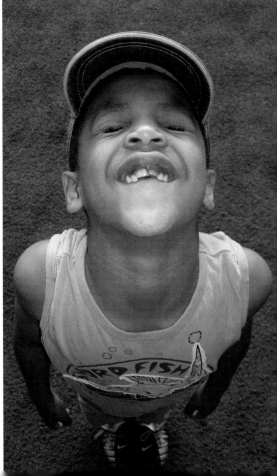

About Interlink Publishing

Established in 1987, Interlink Publishing is an independent publishing house specializing in world travel, fiction-in-translation, history and current affairs, illustrated gift books, international cookbooks, and children's books from around the world. Interlink publishes approximately 50 titles each year and has an active backlist of over 1000 titles under five imprints:

Interlink Books

Interlink Books publishes a general trade list of adult fiction and non-fiction with an emphasis on books that have a wide appeal while also meeting high intellectual and literary standards. Series include:

- The Traveller's History Series
- The Traveller's Wine Guides
- Lost & Found: Classic Travel Writing
- Interlink World Fiction Series
- Interlink Illustrated Histories
- International Folk Tale Series
- Cultural Histories Series
- 100 Best Paintings Series
- Café Life Series
- Eastern Art Series
- Interlink Dive Guides

Olive Branch Press

Olive Branch Press publishes socially and politically relevant non-fiction, concentrating on topics and areas of the world often ignored by the Western media. Titles also include works on a wide range of contemporary issues such as Middle East studies, African studies, women's studies, religion and translated works by academics of international stature.

Cadogan Guides, U.S.A

Cadogan Guides offer twenty years of experience and over a hundred destinations covered. Known for their outstanding research, practical advice, and individual point of view, Cadogan Guides are perfect for the culturally minded, independent traveler.

Clockroot Books

Clockroot Books publishes innovative fiction from around the world. Please visit www.clockrootbooks.com for a complete list of titles under this imprint.

Crocodile Books

Crocodile Books publishes high-quality illustrated children's books from around the world. Titles published under this imprint include quality picture books for preschoolers, as well as fiction and non-fiction books for children ages 3-8.

To order a free copy of our 48-page, full-color catalog visit our website at www.interlinkbooks.com, call us toll-free at 1-800-238-LINK, or write to us at Interlink Publishing, 46 Crosby Street, Northampton, Massachusetts 01060.

Index